SOUPS
— AND —
STEWS

By BARBARA GRUNES

Compliments Of

 **WORLD SAVINGS**®

ideals®

Ideals Publishing Corp.
Nashville, Tennessee

CONTENTS

ISBN 0-8249-3043-6
Copyright © MCMLXXXVIII By Ideals Publishing Corporation.
All rights reserved.
Printed and bound in the United States of America.
Published by
Ideals Publishing Corporation
Nelson Place at Elm Hill Pike
Nashville, Tennessee

Cover Photo:
Mussel Soup, page 34

Onion Soup I, page 5

SUMMER SOUPS

Watercress Soup

Makes 6 servings

3 tablespoons butter
1 onion, chopped
4 stalks celery, sliced
2 leeks, sliced
1 bunch watercress, reserve a few
    leaves for garnish
2 potatoes, peeled and sliced
3 cups chicken stock
½ teaspoon salt
¼ teaspoon white pepper
1 cup heavy cream
    Diced ham

Melt butter in a heavy saucepan; sauté onion, celery and leeks, stirring often, until tender. Add watercress, potatoes, stock, salt and pepper. Cover with water and simmer, covered, until tender, about 20 minutes. Cool soup; remove and purée vegetables and return to soup. Stir in heavy cream and reheat soup gently. Garnish with watercress leaves and diced ham.

Cream of Mushroom Soup

Makes 6 servings

5 tablespoons butter
1 pound mushrooms, sliced
1 quart chicken stock
3 tablespoons butter
3 tablespoons flour
2 cups heavy cream *or*
    half-and-half
½ teaspoon salt
¼ teaspoon white pepper
4 tablespoons dry sherry
¼ cup chopped chives

Melt butter in a saucepan; sauté mushrooms over medium heat, stirring often. Add stock and simmer, covered, for 15 minutes. Drain mushrooms; reserve stock. Purée mushrooms and return to stock. In a small saucepan, melt butter; whisk in flour until absorbed. Stir in 1 cup of the soup and cook until thickened; return to soup. Add cream and season to taste. Stir in sherry and sprinkle soup with chives.

Corn Soup

Makes 6 servings

2 cans (16 ounces each) creamed
    corn
1 quart chicken stock
1 cup heavy cream
½ teaspoon paprika
½ teaspoon salt
¼ teaspoon white pepper
2 tomatoes, peeled and chopped

Using a blender or food processor fitted with a steel blade, purée corn, stock and cream, in two batches. Season with paprika, salt and pepper. Transfer to a heavy saucepan; heat and serve soup garnished with chopped tomatoes.

Cream of Spinach Soup

Makes 6 servings

3 tablespoons butter
2 cloves garlic, minced
8 green onions, chopped
1 quart chicken stock
2 packages (10 ounces each) chopped frozen spinach, thawed and drained
1 large potato, grated
3 cups half-and-half
Salt
Nutmeg

In a large heavy saucepan, melt butter over medium heat; sauté garlic and onions until tender. Add 1 cup stock, spinach and potato. Simmer, covered, for 15 to 20 minutes. Remove spinach mixture and purée in a blender or a food processor fitted with a steel blade; return to soup. Stir in remaining ingredients and simmer for 10 minutes or until soup is warm. Season to taste.

Onion Soup I

Makes 6 to 8 servings

2 tablespoons vegetable oil
3 tablespoons butter
4 cups thinly sliced onions
½ teaspoon salt
¼ teaspoon freshly ground pepper
¼ teaspoon thyme
3 tablespoons flour
1½ quarts beef stock
½ cup dry vermouth
1 small loaf French bread, sliced and toasted
8 slices Swiss cheese
Parmesan cheese

Heat oil and butter in a large heavy skillet; sauté onions until tender, but do not brown. Sprinkle onions with seasonings and flour; stir until flour is absorbed. Add stock and simmer, partially covered, until onions are cooked. Just before serving, stir in vermouth. Pour soup into individual crocks. Arrange toast and Swiss cheese on soup. Sprinkle generously with Parmesan cheese. Broil until cheese is melted.

Onion Soup II

Makes 6 servings

½ cup butter
5 cups white onions, sliced
¼ cup flour
1½ quarts beef stock
¼ teaspoon salt
¼ teaspoon cayenne pepper
1 egg yolk
½ cup cream
Croutons
Freshly grated Parmesan cheese

Melt butter in a heavy saucepan; sauté onions until tender. Whisk in flour until absorbed. Add stock, salt and cayenne; bring to a boil. Reduce heat and simmer, covered, for 10 minutes. Blend egg yolk and cream; stir in 4 tablespoons soup and return mixture to cooled soup. Reheat gently. Serve with croutons and grated cheese.

Cauliflower Soup

Makes 6 servings

1 medium cauliflower, cut
  into florets, reserve ½ cup,
  chopped, for garnish
2 cups half-and-half
3 tablespoons butter
1 white onion, minced
3 tablespoons flour
¼ teaspoon salt
¼ teaspoon white pepper
1 egg yolk, slightly beaten
½ cup heavy cream
  Grated Romano cheese

In a large pan, cover cauliflower with boiling salted water and cook, uncovered, until tender. Strain; reserve liquid. Purée cauliflower and return to cooking liquid. Stir in half-and-half. Melt butter in small saucepan. Sauté onion over medium heat; whisk in flour, salt and pepper until flour is absorbed. Remove from heat; whisk in egg yolk. Add mixture to cauliflower and simmer until soup thickens. Slowly mix in cream and reheat. Serve in small cups sprinkled with bits of cauliflower and grated cheese.

Pottage St. Germain

Makes 6 servings

1 pound fresh green peas *or* 1 can
  (16 ounces) peas
2 ounces fresh spinach
3 heads Romaine lettuce
1½ quarts water
½ cup heavy cream
1 egg yolk
2 tablespoons butter, cut in pieces
½ teaspoon salt
¼ teaspoon ground fennel
  Dill sprigs, optional

Combine vegetables in a large saucepan and cover with water; simmer for 10 minutes. Remove vegetables with a slotted spoon, purée and return to stock. Combine cream and egg; stir into soup. Add butter, salt and fennel; reheat gently. Garnish with dill sprigs, if desired.

Peanut Soup

Makes 4 servings

3 tablespoons butter
1 stalk celery, chopped
1 small red onion, chopped
2 tablespoons flour
¾ cup chunky peanut butter
2 cups chicken stock
2 cups half-and-half
¾ cup peanuts, chopped

In a medium saucepan, melt butter over medium heat. Sauté celery and onion, stirring occasionally, until tender. Whisk in flour and cook until flour is absorbed. Add peanut butter and stir until smooth. Slowly stir in stock and half-and-half. Simmer, uncovered, for 10 to 12 minutes. Serve in small bowls and sprinkle with chopped peanuts.

Cauliflower Soup, this page

Mushroom and Potato Soup

Makes 6 servings

1½ quarts beef stock
2 carrots, sliced
1 pound mushrooms, sliced
1 large onion, thinly sliced
4 potatoes, peeled and sliced
  Salt and pepper to taste
4 tablespoons butter
3 tablespoons flour
1 teaspoon caraway seed

Combine stock, vegetables, salt and pepper in a saucepan. Bring to a boil over medium heat. Reduce heat and simmer, partially covered, until vegetables are tender, about 30 minutes. Melt butter in saucepan; whisk in flour until absorbed. Stir in ½ cup of the soup and cook until mixture thickens; return to soup. Simmer, stirring occasionally, until slightly thickened, about 5 minutes. Stir in caraway seed and serve hot.

Zucchini and Tomato Soup

Makes 6 servings

4 tablespoons butter
2 cloves garlic, minced
1 onion, minced
4 medium zucchini, diced
3 ripe tomatoes, peeled and chopped
1½ quarts beef stock
¼ teaspoon marjoram
  Cooked rice
  Grated Parmesan cheese

Melt butter in a heavy saucepan. Sauté garlic and onion over medium heat, stirring occasionally, until tender. Add zucchini and sauté until golden. Add tomatoes; simmer for 5 minutes. Blend in stock and marjoram; simmer, partially covered, until zucchini is tender, about 15 minutes. Serve with hot rice and sprinkle with grated cheese.

Cream of Carrot Soup with Citron

Makes 6 servings

3 tablespoons butter
6 large carrots, grated
2 medium onions, chopped
4 cups chicken stock
¾ cup freshly squeezed orange juice
2 tablespoons orange zest
¼ teaspoon salt
¼ teaspoon white pepper
¼ teaspoon nutmeg
1 cup heavy cream
  Lemon slices

Melt butter in a large heavy saucepan over medium heat; sauté vegetables until tender, stirring occasionally. Stir in chicken stock; bring to a boil and reduce heat. Simmer for 12 minutes, until carrots are tender. Remove vegetables with a slotted spoon; cool, purée and return to soup. Blend in remaining ingredients except lemon slices and warm over low heat. Garnish with lemon slices.

Cream of Lettuce Soup

Makes 6 servings

4 cups coarsely chopped lettuce
1 large red onion, thinly sliced
3 cups beef stock
2 tablespoons butter
2 tablespoons flour
2 cups half-and-half
¼ teaspoon salt
¼ teaspoon paprika
  Croutons

Combine lettuce, onion and beef stock in a large saucepan; bring to a boil and reduce heat. Cover and simmer, stirring occasionally, for 20 minutes; cool. Remove and purée vegetables; return to stock. In a separate saucepan, melt butter; whisk in flour until absorbed. Stir in half-and-half and cook slowly until slightly thickened. Blend in puréed mixture and season with salt and paprika. Warm soup and serve with croutons.

Zucchini Soup

Makes 6 servings

3 pounds small zucchini
1 cup cooked chopped ham
1 can (10½ ounces) consommé
¼ teaspoon salt
¼ teaspoon white pepper
¼ teaspoon garlic powder
3 tablespoons minced parsley
  Yogurt
  Chopped chives

Remove and discard ends of zucchini; cut into 1-inch pieces. In a stockpot, combine zucchini and remaining ingredients except yogurt and chives; cover with water. Bring mixture to a boil; reduce heat and simmer, partially covered, for 1 hour or until zucchini is tender. Cool soup slightly; purée and transfer to large saucepan. Reheat purée and top servings with yogurt and chopped chives.

Celery Soup

Makes 6 servings

8 stalks celery, sliced
1 large white onion, sliced
1 quart milk
4 tablespoons butter
4 tablespoons flour
½ teaspoon salt
½ teaspoon crushed tarragon
1 cup heavy cream
  Chopped parsley

Combine celery, onion and 2 cups milk in the top of a double boiler; cook until celery is tender. Remove and purée vegetables; return to milk; set aside. In a saucepan, melt butter; whisk in flour until absorbed. Add seasonings, and whisk into celery mixture. Blend in remaining milk and heat, stirring, until soup thickens. Mix in cream and heat gently. Serve in shallow bowls; sprinkle with chopped parsley.

Cheddar Cheese Soup

Makes 6 servings

1 onion, sliced
1 large carrot, sliced
2 stalks celery, sliced
3 cups chicken stock
2 cups milk
4 tablespoons flour
2 cups grated Cheddar cheese
1 cup popped popcorn

Combine vegetables and stock in a saucepan; cook over medium heat until vegetables are tender. Purée vegetables with stock and return to pan. In a blender or food processor fitted with a steel blade, process milk, flour and cheese. Add cheese mixture to stock; combine. Cook over medium heat, stirring often, until slightly thickened. Sprinkle with popcorn and serve hot.

Cream of Asparagus Soup

Makes 6 servings

3 tablespoons butter
1 medium onion, minced
1 stalk celery, chopped
3 cups chicken stock
2 packages (10 ounces each) frozen asparagus, cooked and drained
Salt and pepper to taste
¼ teaspoon crushed chervil
1 cup heavy cream
¼ cup chopped chives

Melt butter in a large saucepan over medium heat. Add onion and celery; sauté until tender. Add stock and asparagus. Cover and simmer for 10 minutes or until asparagus is tender. Season with salt, pepper and chervil. Remove from heat; strain and discard pulp. Return soup to saucepan. Stir in cream. Reheat gently and garnish with chives.

Tomato-Bread Soup

Makes 6 servings

5 ripe tomatoes, peeled and chopped
2 cloves garlic, minced
1 tablespoon basil
¼ teaspoon salt
¼ teaspoon nutmeg
¼ teaspoon thyme
2 teaspoons freshly squeezed lemon juice
1 quart chicken stock
3 tablespoons olive oil
6 slices Italian bread
Freshly grated Parmesan cheese

Combine tomatoes, garlic, basil, salt, nutmeg, thyme and lemon juice in a saucepan; bring to a boil over medium heat. Reduce heat and simmer, partially covered, for 20 minutes. Remove and cool stewed tomatoes. Purée and return to saucepan. Add chicken stock; simmer for 15 minutes. Heat oil in skillet; brown bread slices on both sides. Float a slice of bread in each serving bowl of soup. Sprinkle with Parmesan cheese.

Blue Cheese Soup

Makes 6 servings

3 tablespoons butter
3 tablespoons flour
3 cups chicken stock
2 cups milk
¼ pound Stilton *or* blue
  cheese, crumbled
1 cup half-and-half
¼ teaspoon salt
¼ teaspoon white pepper
  Chopped chives
  Sliced mushrooms

Melt butter in a saucepan. Whisk in flour. Continue cooking, whisking constantly, until flour is absorbed. Stir in 1 cup stock and cook over medium heat until mixture thickens. Add remaining stock and milk. Simmer for 10 minutes, until slightly thickened. Stir in cheese, half-and-half and season to taste; cook for 5 minutes. Serve garnished with chives and mushrooms.

Spinach-Potato Soup

Makes 6 servings

1 package (10 ounces) frozen
  chopped spinach, room
  temperature
2 cups cooked mashed potatoes
3½ cups half-and-half
1 teaspoon crumbled basil
½ teaspoon salt
½ teaspoon thyme
¼ teaspoon white pepper
1 tablespoon butter
½ cup shredded Swiss cheese

Using paper towels, remove excess moisture from spinach. Purée spinach and potatoes; transfer to a saucepan. Add remaining ingredients except Swiss cheese. Simmer, partially covered, stirring occasionally, for 20 minutes. Garnish with Swiss cheese.

Italian Fennel Soup

Makes 6 servings

1 onion, thinly sliced
1 large leek, sliced
2 large fennel bulbs, thinly sliced
3 large ripe tomatoes, peeled and
  chopped
3 cups chicken stock
¼ teaspoon salt
¼ teaspoon pepper
¼ teaspoon garlic powder
2 cups half-and-half
2 sprigs parsley, chopped

Combine vegetables and stock in a heavy saucepan; simmer, partially covered, stirring occasionally, for 1 hour or until the vegetables are tender. Remove and purée vegetables in a blender; return to stock. Add spices, half-and-half and parsley; blend and warm soup gently.

Eggplant Soup
Makes 6 servings

3 tablespoons butter
1 onion, diced
2 cloves garlic, minced
1 medium eggplant, peeled and cubed
3 stalks celery, sliced
1 green bell pepper, diced
¼ teaspoon thyme
¼ teaspoon salt
¼ teaspoon pepper
2 large tomatoes, peeled and chopped
1 quart chicken stock
Minced parsley

Melt butter in a large saucepan; sauté onion and garlic until tender. Add eggplant, celery and pepper; cook, stirring often, until tender. Season to taste with thyme, salt and pepper. Add tomatoes and cook for 5 minutes. Blend in stock. Serve hot, sprinkled with minced parsley.

Cheese and Egg Drop Soup
Makes 6 servings

3 eggs, beaten
¼ teaspoon salt
4 tablespoons freshly grated Parmesan cheese
4 tablespoons Cream of Wheat
½ teaspoon lemon zest
¼ teaspoon nutmeg
5 cups chicken stock
Lemon slices

Combine eggs and salt; whisk in cheese, Cream of Wheat, zest and nutmeg. Stir in ½ cup stock and let stand 15 minutes. Bring remaining stock to a boil in a large heavy saucepan. Drop tablespoons of egg mixture into soup. Reduce heat and simmer, stirring constantly, for 5 minutes. Serve in individual bowls with lemon slices.

Almond Soup
Makes 4 to 6 servings

½ cup ground almonds
¼ cup butter
¼ cup flour
1 can (10½ ounces) chicken stock
2 cups cream
1 small onion, chopped
¼ teaspoon salt
¼ teaspoon almond extract
2 tablespoons dry sherry
Sliced toasted almonds

Combine almonds and butter in a saucepan; cook over medium heat, stirring constantly, until almonds are lightly golden. Whisk in flour and cook until absorbed. Blend in stock, cream, onion, salt and almond extract. Simmer until mixture thickens; stir in sherry. Serve garnished with sliced almonds.

WINTER SOUPS

Mushroom Soup with Puff Pastry Hat

Makes 6 servings

4 tablespoons butter
1 pound mushrooms, sliced,
   stems discarded
¼ teaspoon caraway seed
¼ teaspoon paprika
1 tablespoon flour
1 quart beef stock
1 cup half-and-half
½ pound puff pastry dough
1 egg
   Chopped fresh dill

Melt butter in large heavy saucepan; sauté mushrooms, caraway seed and paprika until mushrooms are tender. Whisk in flour until absorbed. Add stock and simmer, partially covered, for 20 minutes; cool. Remove and purée mushrooms; return to soup. Stir in half-and-half. Fill 6 small cups almost to the rim with soup.

Roll out puff pastry on lightly floured board to ⅛-inch thickness and cut out 6 circles to fit the cups. Beat egg lightly. Brush cup rims with egg wash and cover with pastry circles; trim. Cut a small air vent in center of each pastry circle. Arrange cups on a cookie sheet. Bake in a preheated 400° oven 20 minutes or until dough is puffed and golden. Sprinkle with dill and serve immediately.

Red Cabbage Soup

Makes 6 servings

2 cloves garlic, minced
2 red onions, thinly sliced
1 quart beef stock
2½ pounds chuck steak,
   cut into 1-inch pieces
¼ green cabbage, shredded
3 cups Burgundy
1 can (16 ounces) tomatoes with
   juice, chopped
1 can (8 ounces) tomato sauce
1 medium red cabbage, shredded
¼ cup red wine vinegar
½ teaspoon salt
¼ teaspoon pepper
¼ teaspoon marjoram
   Sliced mushrooms, optional

Combine first 8 ingredients in a stockpot; bring to a boil. Reduce heat and simmer, partially covered, for 1 hour. Stir in red cabbage and vinegar; simmer, partially covered, 1½ hours, or until meat is soft and cabbage is tender. Season with salt, pepper and marjoram. Ladle into deep bowls and garnish with mushrooms, if desired.

Mushroom Soup with Puff
Pastry Hat, this page

Watercress and Potato Soup

Makes 6 servings

4 tablespoons butter
3 leeks, white part only, sliced
1 white onion, minced
3 large potatoes, diced
1 parsnip, diced
1 quart strained chicken stock
¼ teaspoon salt
¼ teaspoon white pepper
1 bunch watercress, chopped
4 tablespoons cooked chopped
   spinach
¼ teaspoon chervil
1 cup heavy cream
   Watercress sprigs

Melt butter in a stockpot; sauté leeks and onion, stirring often, until tender. Stir in potatoes, parsnip and stock; cover and cook over low heat for 20 minutes or until tender. Remove and purée vegetables; return to soup. Season with salt and pepper. Combine watercress, spinach and chervil in a small saucepan; stir in 1 cup of hot soup. Mix in ½ cup boiling water. Cover and simmer for 10 minutes or until tender; purée. Blend together ¼ cup cream and watercress mixture; cover and refrigerate until ready to serve. Blend remaining cream with soup; cover and refrigerate. When serving, place potato soup in a deep tureen. Drop spoonfuls of watercress mixture on surface of soup. To create marbling, gently swirl watercress into soup. Garnish with watercress sprigs.

Minestrone

Makes 8 servings

3 tablespoons bacon drippings
1 cup chopped Italian sausage
1 large onion, sliced
1 carrot, sliced
1 stalk celery, sliced
2 large tomatoes, peeled and
   chopped
1 large potato, diced
1 can (16 ounces) tomatoes
   with juice, crushed
1 cup sliced zucchini
½ small head cabbage, shredded
1 can (15½ ounces) undrained red
   kidney beans *or* garbanzos
1½ quarts beef stock
1 tablespoon crushed dried basil
1 clove garlic, minced
½ teaspoon salt
2 cups cooked elbow macaroni
   Grated Parmesan cheese

Heat bacon drippings in large heavy skillet; fry sausage and onion over medium heat until tender. Transfer to a stockpot. Add vegetables, kidney beans and stock. Cover and simmer for 15 minutes. Add seasonings and macaroni. Simmer, stirring occasionally, until soup thickens and all ingredients are cooked. Serve hot sprinkled with grated cheese.

Black Bean and Ham Soup

Makes 8 servings

12 ounces dry black beans
 1 smoked ham bone *or* 1 cup
   chopped cooked ham
 4 strips bacon, cut into 1-inch
   pieces
 3 stalks celery, chopped
 2 onions, thinly sliced
 1 large leek, thinly sliced
 3 bay leaves
 1 teaspoon salt
 ½ teaspoon freshly ground pepper
 ½ teaspoon cumin
 ¼ cup dry sherry
   Chopped hard-boiled eggs
   Chopped onions

Cover beans with water and soak overnight; drain. In a large heavy saucepan, cover beans with 2 quarts water. Add ham bone; bring to a boil over high heat. Reduce heat and simmer, partially covered, for 2 hours or until beans are tender. Add additional water if necessary. Sauté bacon in large skillet. Add remaining ingredients except sherry, eggs and onions, stirring occasionally, until tender. Add additional water, if necessary. Add vegetable mixture to beans and cook until beans are tender. Discard ham bone and bay leaves. Remove and purée beans and vegetables. Return to pot. Add 2 cups water, or to desired thickness; reheat. Stir in sherry to taste and serve garnished with eggs and onions.

Soup with Pistou

Makes 6 servings

 3 tomatoes, peeled and chopped
 ¾ pound green beans, cut into
   1½-inch pieces
 3 large potatoes, cubed
 1 teaspoon salt
 ¼ teaspoon pepper
   Pistou
 2 cups cooked spaghetti
   Grated Gruyere *or* Swiss cheese
   Flavored croutons

Combine tomatoes, beans and potatoes in a large heavy saucepan; add 1½ quarts water. Season with salt and pepper. Bring soup to a boil, reduce heat and simmer, partially covered, for 45 minutes. Prepare Pistou and set aside. Add spaghetti to soup and heat. To serve, remove 1 cup of the stock to a serving bowl, stir in 1 teaspoon of the Pistou. Ladle vegetables and spaghetti over soup. Sprinkle with cheese and croutons. Repeat for each serving and serve hot.

Pistou

Makes ½ cup

 ½ cup fresh basil leaves, chopped
 3 cloves garlic, crushed
 ¼ cup olive oil

Combine all ingredients and purée; set aside.

17

Harvest Pepper Soup

Makes 6 servings

3 tablespoons butter
2 onions, chopped
1½ quarts chicken stock
8 red bell peppers, cut into pieces
1 cup milk
½ teaspoon salt
½ teaspoon thyme
½ teaspoon garlic powder
1 cup heavy cream
1 green bell pepper, sliced

Melt butter in a Dutch oven over medium heat; sauté onions until tender. Add stock and peppers; cover and cook for 15 minutes. Cool soup. Remove and purée vegetables; return to soup. Stir in milk and seasonings; simmer for 10 minutes. Cool slightly. Slowly stir in cream and serve warm garnished with green pepper slices.

Senate Bean Soup

Makes 8 servings

3 tablespoons butter
2 large onions, diced
4 stalks celery, sliced
½ pound navy beans, soaked overnight in 1½ quarts water
2 quarts beef stock
½ pound ham, chopped
½ pound potatoes, sliced
½ teaspoon salt
¼ teaspoon pepper
¼ teaspoon thyme

Melt butter in a stockpot; sauté onions and celery until tender. Add beans, stock, ham and potatoes; simmer, partially covered, for 3 hours, stirring occasionally. Add water as necessary during cooking. Season with salt, pepper and thyme; simmer, uncovered, for 15 minutes. Serve hot.

Pea Soup

Makes 8 servings

3 tablespoons butter
2 onions, minced
3 potatoes, diced
2 pounds fresh green peas, shelled and cooked *or* 3 packages (10 ounces each) frozen peas, cooked
2 tablespoons butter
¼ teaspoon chopped mint leaves
Salt and white pepper to taste
2 cups milk
1 cup heavy cream
Mint leaves

Melt butter in a large saucepan; sauté onions until tender. Add potatoes and 1 cup boiling water. Cover and cook until potatoes are tender, about 15 minutes. Remove and purée vegetables; return to saucepan with butter, mint, salt and pepper. Stir in milk over low heat until soup is of desired consistency. Slowly add cream and heat gently, but do not boil. Serve warm garnished with mint leaves.

18

Dried Mushroom Soup

Makes 6 servings

¼ pound dried mushrooms (European variety), reconstituted in 1 quart water
1 quart chicken stock
4 tablespoons butter
2 large white onions, diced
3 tablespoons flour
½ teaspoon salt
½ teaspoon rosemary
¼ teaspoon black pepper
2 cups cooked barley

Strain mushrooms through a double layer of cheesecloth; reserve 1 quart liquid. Slice mushrooms thinly. Add mushrooms, reserved liquid and stock to a saucepan and simmer for 1 hour or until reduced by half. Melt butter in a skillet; sauté onions, stirring often, until tender. Whisk in flour until absorbed. Add 1 cup of mushroom soup and continue cooking until thickened; return to soup. Stir in seasonings and barley. Heat soup and serve.

Cheese Chowder

Makes 6 servings

2 large potatoes, diced
1 large carrot, sliced
2 stalks celery, sliced
1 small onion, minced
½ teaspoon salt
¼ teaspoon white pepper
4 tablespoons butter
4 tablespoons flour
2 cups milk
2 cups shredded Cheddar cheese
2 cans (17 ounces each) creamed corn

Combine vegetables and seasonings in a heavy saucepan; add 2 cups boiling water. Bring mixture to a boil; reduce heat and simmer, partially covered, for 10 minutes. Melt butter in a separate saucepan; whisk in flour over medium heat until absorbed. Whisk in milk and cook until sauce thickens. Stir in cheese until melted. Add sauce and creamed corn to vegetables. Heat gently; do not boil.

Garlic Soup

Makes 6 servings

4 tablespoons butter
8 cloves garlic, crushed
2 tablespoons flour
1½ quarts chicken stock
2 drops Tabasco Sauce
¼ teaspoon salt
¼ teaspoon pepper
6 eggs
4 tablespoons chopped broad-leaf parsley
¼ cup crumbled corn chips

In a large heavy saucepan, melt butter over medium heat; stir in garlic and flour until the garlic is tender and the flour is absorbed. Stir in stock; bring to a boil. Reduce heat and simmer, covered, for 10 minutes. Add Tabasco and seasonings. Poach eggs gently, by sliding into the simmering soup. Ladle soup into bowls. Sprinkle with parsley and crumbled chips.

Philadelphia Pepper Soup

Makes 6 servings

3 potatoes, sliced
4 green bell peppers, sliced
½ pound small white onions, sliced
1 quart chicken stock
4 tablespoons butter
¼ teaspoon salt
¼ teaspoon pepper
¼ teaspoon nutmeg
2 cups heavy cream *or*
   half-and-half
   Chopped pepper

Combine potatoes, peppers and onions in a saucepan. Add 2 cups stock or enough to cover. Bring mixture to a boil; reduce heat and simmer, partially covered, until tender, about 15 minutes. Purée mixture and return to saucepan. Add remaining ingredients except cream and chopped pepper. Simmer, stirring often, until soup is warm. Fold in cream and heat slowly. Sprinkle with chopped pepper and serve.

Pumpkin Buttermilk Soup

Makes 6 servings

3 tablespoons butter
1 onion, minced
3 tablespoons flour
1 can (16 ounces) pumpkin purée
½ teaspoon ginger
¼ teaspoon salt
¼ teaspoon white pepper
¼ teaspoon nutmeg
¼ teaspoon pumpkin pie spice
3 cups chicken stock
2 cups buttermilk
   Medium pumpkin, optional
   Chopped candied ginger

Melt butter in a large heavy saucepan. Sauté onion, stirring often, until tender. Whisk in flour until absorbed. Blend in remaining ingredients except buttermilk and candied ginger. Bring soup to a boil; reduce heat and simmer for 10 minutes. Stir in buttermilk and warm soup. Pour into individual bowls or serve from a medium seeded pumpkin, if desired. Sprinkle with candied ginger.

Cabbage Soup

Makes 6 servings

1 small head cabbage, shredded
2 onions, thinly sliced
1 can (28 ounces) tomatoes with
   juice, chopped
½ teaspoon salt
¼ teaspoon pepper
3 tablespoons freshly squeezed
   lemon juice
½ cup light brown sugar
3 cups tomato juice *or* water
1 lemon, thinly sliced

Cover cabbage with water in a large pot; bring to a boil. Reduce heat and simmer, partially covered, stirring occasionally, for 30 minutes or until cabbage is cooked. Drain and return cabbage to pot. Stir in remaining ingredients except lemon slices. Cover with tomato juice or water. Simmer for 1 hour or until tender, adding extra liquid, as necessary. Serve with floating lemon slices.

Turkey Stuffing Soup
Makes 6 servings

4 tablespoons butter
1 large red onion, chopped
3 carrots, thinly sliced
3 stalks celery, sliced
2 large tomatoes, peeled and chopped
3 to 4 cups chopped cooked turkey
3 sprigs parsley, minced
1½ quarts turkey *or* beef stock
2 cups leftover turkey stuffing
1½ cups cooked pasta bows *or* alphabet noodles

In a stockpot over low heat, melt butter. Sauté onion, carrots and celery until tender. Stir in tomatoes, turkey and parsley. Add stock and stuffing. Bring soup to a boil; reduce heat and simmer, partially covered, for 1 hour. Place hot noodles in a large deep bowl; cover with soup.

Mushroom Barley Soup
Makes 8 servings

¾ cup navy beans
½ cup green split peas
¼ cup yellow split peas
½ cup barley
2 pounds short ribs
1 pound mushrooms, sliced
1 onion, thinly sliced
1 large carrot, sliced

Prepare soup one day in advance. Combine all ingredients in a stockpot; cover with water. Bring mixture to a boil over medium heat. Reduce heat and simmer, partially covered, for 2 hours or until cooked. Skim soup and add additional water as necessary.

Hearty Steak Soup
Makes 6 servings

¾ pound roughly ground beefsteak
3 tablespoons butter
3 tablespoons flour
3 cans (10½ ounces each) consommé
1 large carrot, grated
1 large onion, minced
2 stalks celery, sliced
1 large tomato, peeled and chopped
½ teaspoon Kitchen Bouquet
1 can (16 ounces) mixed vegetables, drained

Brown beef in a hot skillet; drain. Melt butter in a large saucepan over medium heat. Whisk in flour until absorbed. Add consommé and cook until mixture thickens and comes to a boil. Add browned beef and remaining ingredients; simmer for 10 minutes. Serve hot.

Hearty Steak Soup, this page

Hot and Sour Soup

Makes 6 to 8 servings

3 tablespoons cloud ear
   mushrooms
3 tablespoons golden needles
1 quart chicken stock
1 tablespoon light soy sauce
¼ teaspoon salt
½ pound bean curd, cut into
   ½-inch pieces
½ cup canned shredded bamboo
   shoots, drained
2 tablespoons cornstarch
3 tablespoons red wine vinegar
¼ teaspoon black pepper
1 teaspoon sesame oil
3 eggs, slightly beaten
4 green onions, minced

Cover mushrooms and golden needles with hot water. Allow to stand 20 minutes; drain and chop. Heat stock, soy sauce and salt in a large heavy saucepan. Stir in mushrooms, golden needles, bean curd and bamboo shoots; cook over medium heat for 1 minute. Blend cornstarch and 4 tablespoons of hot chicken stock; stir into soup and cook over medium heat until soup thickens slightly. Add vinegar, pepper and sesame oil. Bring soup to a boil. In a slow steady stream, stir in beaten eggs. Turn heat off, wait 1 minute, and stir soup until egg drops form. Garnish soup with green onions and serve in oriental bowls.

Vegetable Soup with Meatballs

Makes 8 servings

2 tablespoons butter
2 tablespoons olive oil
1 onion, chopped
1 stalk celery, sliced
1 clove garlic, minced
1 can (16 ounces) tomatoes with
   juice, crushed
1 can (6 ounces) tomato paste
   Meatballs
1 cup canned chick peas, drained
1 cup canned kidney beans,
   drained
1 cup cooked, chopped spinach,
   drained
2 teaspoons minced parsley
1 carrot, sliced
½ teaspoon salt
½ teaspoon oregano
½ teaspoon basil
1½ cups cooked spaghetti, cut into
   small pieces
   Chopped tomatoes

In a stockpot, heat butter and olive oil; sauté onion, celery and garlic over medium heat, until tender. Stir in tomatoes, tomato paste and 1 quart water. Bring mixture to a boil; gently add Meatballs. Reduce heat and simmer for 25 to 30 minutes, until Meatballs have cooked. Add remaining ingredients except chopped tomatoes. Cover and simmer 10 minutes. Garnish with chopped tomatoes.

Meatballs

1 **pound ground chuck**
½ **cup fine bread crumbs**
¼ **cup freshly grated Parmesan cheese**
1 **egg, slightly beaten**
1 **clove garlic, minced**
3 **green onions, chopped**
½ **teaspoon salt**

Combine all ingredients. Shape into walnut-sized meatballs.

Lentil Soup
Makes 6 to 8 servings

4 **tablespoons olive oil** *or* **butter**
1 **large onion, thinly sliced**
4 **stalks celery, chopped**
1 **large carrot, thinly sliced**
2 **potatoes, cubed**
1½ **quarts water**
1 **pound assorted lentils**
1 **tablespoon tomato sauce**
2 **bay leaves**
½ **cup red wine**
½ **teaspoon oregano**
1 **teaspoon salt**
¼ **teaspoon freshly ground pepper**
   Dark bread

Heat olive oil in a stockpot over medium heat. Sauté onion, celery, carrot and potatoes until tender. Add water, lentils, tomato sauce and bay leaves; bring to a boil. Reduce heat and simmer, covered, for 1½ hours. Add water as necessary. When lentils are cooked, remove bay leaves; add wine and remaining seasonings. Serve with hearty dark bread.

Black Bean Soup
Makes 8 servings

1 **pound black beans**
3 **tablespoons bacon drippings**
2 **medium onions, chopped**
1 **stalk celery, sliced**
4 **cloves garlic, minced**
1 **quart chicken stock**
½ **teaspoon salt**
¼ **teaspoon black pepper**
2 **teaspoons chili powder**
2 **teaspoons cumin**
1 **cup cream**
   Chopped green onions
   Sour cream

Cover beans with water and soak overnight. Heat bacon drippings in large heavy saucepan and sauté onions, celery and garlic, stirring occasionally, until tender. Stir in beans, stock and seasonings. Bring soup to a boil; reduce heat and simmer, partially covered, for 1½ hours. Add additional stock or water to keep beans covered. Beans should be tender. Cool slightly; purée. Return soup to pot and blend in cream. Heat gently and serve in deep bowls sprinkled with onions and topped with sour cream.

CHICKEN STOCK BASED SOUPS

Zuppa Pavese

Makes 6 servings

1½ quarts chicken stock
Salt and pepper to taste
3 tablespoons minced parsley
6 eggs
6 slices white bread, toasted, discard crusts
Freshly grated Parmesan cheese

In a large skillet, combine stock, salt, pepper and parsley; bring to a boil. Reduce heat and simmer. Carefully add eggs to stock, one at a time. Poach and remove with slotted spoon; keep warm. Strain stock and divide into 6 bowls. Arrange a toast slice on soup and top with an egg. Sprinkle with cheese.

Chicken Lemon Soup

Makes 6 servings

1½ quarts chicken stock
½ teaspoon salt
¼ teaspoon white pepper
3 tablespoons chopped parsley
1 cup cooked rice
4 tablespoons freshly squeezed lemon juice
4 eggs, lightly beaten

Combine stock, salt, pepper, parsley and rice in a medium saucepan; bring to a boil over medium heat. Reduce heat and simmer. Slowly sprinkle lemon juice into eggs and add ½ cup of the warm stock. In a slow steady stream, add egg mixture to soup, stirring constantly. Serve immediately.

Chicken Vegetable Soup

Makes 6 servings

3 tablespoons butter
2 medium onions, thinly sliced
1 green bell pepper, sliced
1 large carrot, sliced
2 stalks celery, sliced
1 turnip, diced
1 parsnip, sliced
½ chicken, cut in pieces
4 chicken bouillon cubes
3 sprigs parsley, chopped
Salt and pepper to taste

Melt butter in a stockpot; lightly sauté vegetables. Add remaining ingredients and 1½ quarts water; bring to a boil over medium heat. Reduce heat and simmer, partially covered, stirring occasionally, for 1½ hours. Season with salt and pepper. Serve with warm noodles or rice.

South of the Border Chicken Soup

Makes 6 servings

¼ **pound bacon, cut into 2-inch pieces**
2 **medium onions, chopped**
1 **cup cubed cooked chicken**
1 **can (3 ounces) chopped mild green chilies, drained**
1 **quart chicken stock**
12 **corn tortillas, cut into wedges**
¼ **pound grated Monterey Jack cheese**

In a large heavy saucepan, fry bacon and onions over medium heat until crisp. Stir in chicken, green chilies and stock. Warm over medium heat and sprinkle with tortillas and grated cheese.

Chicken Soup with Tofu

Makes 6 servings

1 **quart chicken stock**
½ **pound tofu, cut into ½-inch pieces**
½ **pound spinach, chopped**
½ **teaspoon salt**
¼ **teaspoon white pepper**
½ **teaspoon sesame oil**
1 **teaspoon soy sauce**
2 **tablespoons cornstarch**
2 **egg whites, lightly beaten**

In a saucepan, bring stock to a boil. Stir in tofu, spinach, seasonings, oil and soy sauce. In a small bowl, combine cornstarch with 4 tablespoons of the chicken stock; return to soup and cook over medium heat until slightly thickened. Slowly stir in egg whites. Serve soup in small bowls.

Chicken Noodle Soup

Makes 6 servings

1 **3½-pound chicken, quartered**
2 **chicken bouillon cubes**
1 **tablespoon chopped fresh dillweed**
1 **tablespoon chopped fresh parsley**
  Salt and pepper to taste
2 **stalks celery with leaves, sliced**
2 **carrots, sliced**
1 **onion, quartered**
1 **large parsnip, sliced**
  Cooked noodles

Bring 3 quarts of water to a boil in a stockpot. Add all ingredients except noodles. Cook, partially covered, over medium-low heat for 1½ hours. Remove chicken and discard bones. Remove vegetables and slice or purée. Strain soup through a double layer of cheesecloth. Return chicken and vegetables to soup; reheat. Ladle soup over noodles in shallow bowls.

Note: Chicken soup tastes best when prepared a day in advance.

Oriental Winter Melon Soup

Makes 6 servings

¼ cup dried Chinese mushrooms,
    reconstituted in hot water
1 pound winter melon
½ cup diced cooked chicken
¼ cup diced cooked ham
5 cups chicken stock
¼ cup sliced bamboo shoots
¼ teaspoon salt
¼ teaspoon pepper
¼ teaspoon ginger
    Chopped broadleaf parsley

Discard mushroom stems and slice. Remove melon skin and discard seeds; cut into ½-inch pieces. Combine all ingredients except parsley in a large saucepan and bring to a boil. Reduce heat and simmer, partially covered, for 20 minutes. Ladle into small bowls and sprinkle with parsley.

Mulligatawny Soup

Makes 6 servings

4 tablespoons butter
2 medium onions, quartered
4 large tomatoes, peeled and
    chopped
1 potato, sliced
2 cups cooked turkey
1½ quarts beef stock
1 teaspoon curry powder
½ teaspoon Worcestershire sauce
    Salt and pepper
1 large apple, grated
    Cooked rice

Melt butter in a heavy saucepan; sauté onion until tender. Stir in tomatoes, potato, turkey, stock, curry and Worcestershire sauce. Bring soup to a boil. Reduce heat and simmer, partially covered, stirring occasionally, for 30 minutes. Season to taste, sprinkle with grated apple and serve with cooked rice.

Cock-a-Leekie Soup

Makes 6 servings

3 tablespoons butter
4 large leeks, white part only,
    sliced
3 potatoes, diced
1 large onion, minced
3 cups chicken stock
2 cups milk
1 cup heavy cream
    Salt and white pepper
    Chopped chives

In a large heavy saucepan, melt butter and sauté leeks, potatoes and onion, stirring often, until onions are tender. Cover and simmer for 15 minutes. Stir in stock and milk; cover and cook 5 minutes. Cool slightly; remove and purée vegetables. Return vegetables to soup; add cream and season with salt and pepper. Warm and serve garnished with chives.

BISQUE, CHOWDER AND FISH SOUPS

Cioppino
Makes 8 servings

¼ cup olive oil
3 tablespoons butter
2 onions, thinly sliced
4 cloves garlic, minced
½ pound mushrooms, sliced
1 green bell pepper, sliced
1 can (28 ounces) plum tomatoes
with juice
1 can (6 ounces) tomato paste
2 tablespoons dried basil
1 tablespoon orange zest
1 tablespoon freshly ground
pepper
2 cups dry wine
2 pounds cod, red snapper *or*
halibut
¾ pound scallops
1 pound mussels *or* clams,
debearded
¾ pound medium shrimp, shelled
and deveined
Orange slices
Sliced sourdough bread

Heat olive oil and butter in a stockpot over medium heat; sauté onion and garlic until tender. Add mushrooms and green pepper; sauté until soft. Stir in tomatoes, tomato paste, spices and wine; simmer, covered, for 20 minutes. Stir in fish and scallops. Add additional wine to cover, if necessary; cook 10 minutes. Add mussels and shrimp. Cover and cook until clams open; discard any unopened shells. Serve from soup tureen with orange slices and sourdough bread.

Oyster-Spinach Soup
Makes 6 servings

2 cups milk
2 cups half-and-half
10 fresh oysters, shucked and
puréed
¾ cup cooked spinach, puréed
2 cloves garlic, minced
¼ teaspoon salt
¼ teaspoon white pepper
1 tablespoon cornstarch
Croutons

Heat milk and half-and-half in a medium saucepan over low heat. Stir in remaining ingredients except cornstarch and croutons. Simmer for 10 minutes. Whisk together ½ cup hot soup and cornstarch; return to soup. Simmer until soup thickens slightly. Serve with croutons.

Pimiento Bisque

Makes 6 servings

3 tablespoons butter
1 onion, minced
3 tablespoons flour
2 cups milk
¾ cup pimiento, drained and
   puréed
¼ teaspoon salt
¼ teaspoon white pepper
½ teaspoon tarragon
2 cups heavy cream
   Chopped red bell pepper

Melt butter in a large heavy saucepan; sauté onion until tender. Whisk in flour until absorbed. Add milk, whisking constantly, until soup thickens. Add pimiento and seasonings; warm. Blend in cream and warm. Serve in small bowls and sprinkle with chopped pepper.

Shrimp Bisque

Makes 6 servings

1½ pounds raw shrimp, shelled and
   deveined
5 tablespoons butter
1 small onion, minced
1 stalk celery, sliced
1 small carrot, sliced
3 cups chicken stock
¼ teaspoon thyme
¼ teaspoon salt
1 cup heavy cream
4 tablespoons dry sherry
   Unsweetened whipped cream
   Chopped chives

Grind shrimp in a food processor fitted with a steel blade. Melt butter in a saucepan and sauté onion, celery and carrot until tender. Add shrimp and cook for 5 minutes, stirring often. Add stock, thyme and salt; simmer, partially covered, for 30 minutes. Strain soup, forcing the pulp through sieve. Stir in cream and sherry. Reheat gently. Serve in small bowls and top with whipped cream and chives.

Oyster Stew

Makes 6 servings

1 quart oysters with liquid
2 stalks celery, sliced
2 slices crusty bread, toasted
¼ teaspoon salt
¼ teaspoon white pepper
¼ teaspoon nutmeg
4 tablespoons butter
3 tablespoons flour
3 cups milk
1 cup heavy cream
   Unsweetened whipped cream

Heat oysters with liquid in a large saucepan over medium heat; *do not boil.* Cool; strain and reserve liquid. Grind oysters, celery and bread. Stir in the reserved liquid and seasonings. Melt butter in a small saucepan; whisk in flour until absorbed. Add 1 cup milk and cook until the mixture thickens; add to oysters. Blend in remaining milk and cream; simmer until stew thickens. Serve hot with whipped cream.

Smoked Cod Chowder

Makes 6 servings

3 tablespoons butter
2 medium onions, thinly sliced
1½ pounds finnan haddie, cut into
   2-inch pieces
1 large carrot, diced
3 large potatoes, diced
1 quart milk
2 tablespoons butter
¼ teaspoon salt
¼ teaspoon white pepper
   Oyster crackers

Melt butter in a large saucepan. Add onions and sauté. Add fish, vegetables and water to cover. Cook, uncovered, over medium heat until fish is tender, about 30 minutes. Discard fish bones. Reserve 2 cups liquid and the vegetables; stir in remaining ingredients except crackers. Simmer, uncovered, until chowder is warm. Serve from soup tureen with oyster crackers.

Easy Crab Soup

Makes 6 to 8 servings

2 cans (10½ ounces each) cream
   of celery soup
1 cup crabmeat, drained
2 cloves garlic, minced
3 cups milk
1 cup heavy cream
3 hard-boiled eggs, chopped
4 tablespoons butter, cut into
   pieces
   Dash Worcestershire sauce
¼ teaspoon white pepper
   Sherry to taste
   Slivered toasted almonds

In a large saucepan, combine all ingredients except sherry and almonds. Bring soup to a boil over medium-low heat, stirring occasionally. Stir in sherry; ladle into shallow bowls and sprinkle with almonds.

Bookbinder Soup

Makes 6 servings

3 tablespoons butter
1 large onion, thinly sliced
1 large green bell pepper, diced
3 stalks celery, sliced
2 tomatoes, peeled and chopped
1 pound red snapper fillets, cut
   into 1-inch strips
1 quart fish stock
1½ cups tomato sauce
1 cup dry sherry
   Buttered croutons

Melt butter in a large heavy saucepan over medium heat. Sauté onion, pepper and celery until tender, stirring occasionally. Stir in tomatoes and fish; cook 3 to 4 minutes. Add stock and tomato sauce; bring to a boil. Reduce heat and stir in sherry; simmer 4 to 5 minutes. Serve in small bowls with croutons.

Fast Salmon Chowder

Makes 6 servings

2 cans (7¾ ounces each) salmon
   with liquid
2 cans (10¾ ounces each)
   condensed tomato soup
2 cups milk
1 can (16 ounces) cream-style
   corn
¼ teaspoon curry powder
¼ teaspoon ginger
1 lime, sliced

In a medium saucepan, combine all ingredients except sliced lime. Cook over medium heat, stirring constantly, until soup is smooth and heated; *do not boil.* Serve with lime slices.

Clam Chowder

Makes 6 servings

1 large onion, thinly sliced
1 pound potatoes, diced
1 pint fresh clams *or* 3 cans
   (6½ ounces each) minced clams
   with liquid
1 pint half-and-half *or* milk
3 tablespoons butter
   Crackers

Cover vegetables with water in a large saucepan. Cook over medium heat, partially covered, until vegetables are tender, stirring occasionally. Stir in clams and simmer 5 minutes. Add half-and-half and butter; heat and serve with crackers.

Mussel Soup

Makes 6 to 8 servings

1½ pounds mussels, debearded,
      soaked 1 hour and drained
  2 cups dry white wine
  1 small onion, sliced
  3 sprigs parsley, minced
  3 tablespoons butter, cut in pieces
  4 tablespoons olive oil
  2 onions, sliced
  2 leeks, white part only, sliced
1½ cups fish stock
  2 tomatoes, peeled and chopped
  ¼ teaspoon thyme
  ¼ teaspoon garlic powder
  ¼ teaspoon salt
  ¼ teaspoon white pepper
  1 cup half-and-half *or* heavy
      cream
      Dash saffron, optional
      Crusty bread

Combine mussels, wine, onion, parsley and butter in a stockpot; bring to a boil. Reduce heat and simmer, covered, for 10 minutes. Discard any unopened mussels. Heat oil in a large saucepan. Sauté onion and leeks until tender. Add stock, tomatoes and seasonings. Simmer for 30 minutes. Add mussels with broth, half-and-half and saffron, if desired; simmer for 2 minutes. Serve in deep bowls with crusty bread.

34

Mussel Soup, this page

STEWS

New Orleans Gumbo

Makes 8 servings

¼ cup bacon drippings
5 tablespoons flour
2 tablespoons butter
2 cloves garlic, minced
1 large onion, chopped
2 stalks celery, sliced
1 red bell pepper, sliced
1 quart chicken stock
1 can (28 ounces) tomatoes with juice, crushed
1 can (6 ounces) tomato paste
¼ teaspoon thyme
¼ teaspoon rosemary
¼ teaspoon oregano
2 bay leaves
1 teaspoon salt
¼ teaspoon freshly ground pepper
Tabasco sauce to taste
1½ pounds firm-fleshed fish fillets, cut into 1-inch pieces
¾ pound shrimp, peeled and deveined
1 package (10 ounces) frozen sliced okra, at room temperature and drained
½ teaspoon gumbo filé
4 cups cooked rice

Heat bacon drippings in a saucepan over medium heat. Whisk in flour until it turns a deep rich brown; set aside. In a stockpot or Dutch oven, melt butter and sauté garlic, onion, celery and pepper, stirring occasionally, until tender. Stir in stock, tomatoes, tomato paste, seasonings and flour mixture. Simmer, partially covered, about 20 minutes. Stir in fish, shrimp and okra. Cover and cook 10 minutes or until the shrimp is cooked. Remove pot from heat and stir in filé. (Do not reheat soup once the filé has been added.) Serve soup with hot rice.

Wisconsin Fish Boil

Makes 8 servings

16 small red potatoes
½ cup salt
4½ pounds whitefish, head removed, cut into steaks
¼ pound butter, melted
2 lemons, cut into wedges
8 sprigs parsley

Wash and trim potatoes; arrange in a double layer of cheesecloth. Pour water into a stockpot with a removable rack until half-full; add salt. Bring water to a boil over high heat. Cook potatoes 20 minutes. Wrap fish in cheesecloth, secure ends, and arrange in pot. Cook fish 10 minutes; skim. Transfer potatoes and fish to serving platter. Serve with melted butter and lemon wedges; garnish with parsley.

Chicken Gumbo

Makes 8 servings

4 tablespoons peanut oil
1 3½-pound chicken, cut into 8 pieces
1 slice cooked ham, cut into ½-inch pieces
5 tablespoons butter
5 tablespoons flour
2 tablespoons butter
2 cloves garlic, minced
2 large onions, thinly sliced
1 green bell pepper, sliced
½ teaspoon salt
½ teaspoon thyme
½ teaspoon crushed red pepper
¼ teaspoon fennel seed
2 bay leaves
1 can (28 ounces) tomatoes with juice, chopped
1 cup tomato juice
1 package (10 ounces) frozen cut okra, thawed and drained
2 cups chicken stock
Cooked rice

Heat oil in a large heavy saucepan or Dutch oven over medium heat. Sauté chicken until golden; stir in ham. Remove chicken and ham; reserve. Reheat drippings; add 5 tablespoons butter and melt. Whisk in flour until dark and rich; reserve. Heat 2 tablespoons butter in Dutch oven; sauté garlic, onions, pepper and seasonings, stirring occasionally, until tender. Stir in tomatoes, juice, okra, stock and flour mixture. Reduce heat and simmer, partially covered, stirring occasionally, for 30 minutes or until chicken is cooked. Discard bay leaves. Serve with rice.

Fish Stew

Makes 6 servings

1 quart fish stock, clam juice or water
2 pounds firm-fleshed fish, cut into 1½-inch pieces
2 whole leeks, sliced
2 carrots, sliced
2 stalks celery, sliced
1 teaspoon salt
¼ teaspoon white pepper
¼ teaspoon thyme
2 bay leaves
4 tablespoons butter
4 tablespoons flour
1 cup milk
1 egg yolk
1 cup heavy cream
Oyster crackers

Heat fish stock in a large saucepan over medium heat. Add fish, vegetables and seasonings. Reduce heat and simmer 15 minutes or until the vegetables are tender. Melt butter in a small saucepan; whisk in flour until absorbed. Stir in milk and egg yolk over low heat. Whisk in cream and simmer until thickened. Whisk mixture into fish stew; heat. Serve in deep bowls with oyster crackers.

Cincinnati 5-Way Chili

Makes 6 servings

1½ pounds ground beef
½ teaspoon salt
½ teaspoon garlic powder
¼ teaspoon pepper
1 can (8 ounces) tomato sauce
4 tablespoons catsup
1 tablespoon wine vinegar
2 teaspoons chili powder
1 teaspon paprika
½ teaspoon cumin
½ teaspoon marjoram
½ teaspoon allspice
¼ teaspoon cloves
¼ teaspoon coriander
1 bay leaf
1 teaspoon honey
½ ounce unsweetened chocolate, grated
  Tomato juice
1 pound spaghetti, cooked and drained
2 tablespoons butter
1 can (16 ounces) kidney beans, cooked
1 large onion, minced
½ pound Cheddar cheese, grated

Brown meat in a large heavy skillet over high heat. Sprinkle with salt, garlic powder, and pepper. Add tomato sauce, catsup, vinegar and 1 cup hot water. Blend in remaining spices, honey and chocolate. Cover and simmer, stirring occasionally, for 30 minutes. Add tomato juice to desired consistency. Remove and discard bay leaf. Toss spaghetti with butter.

To assemble, transfer spaghetti to serving plates; top with chili. Add a layer of kidney beans and sprinkle with onions. Top with grated cheese.

Beef-Wine Stew

Makes 8 servings

¼ pound bacon, cut into 1-inch pieces
1 pound small white onions, peeled
4 pounds top round beef, cut into 1-inch pieces
4 tablespoons flour
1 bottle (⅘ quart) Burgundy
8 small potatoes, peeled and cubed
4 sprigs parsley, chopped
¼ teaspoon pepper
¼ teaspoon crushed dried tarragon

Fry bacon in a Dutch oven over medium heat. Add onions and sauté until golden brown. Remove bacon and onions; reserve. Reheat drippings. Add beef and brown; sprinkle with flour and continue cooking until absorbed. Add Burgundy and enough water to cover. Return bacon and onions. Add potatoes. Season with parsley, pepper and tarragon. Bring stew to a boil; reduce heat and simmer, partially covered, for 2 hours or until meat is tender.

Cincinnati 5-Way Chili, this page

Atlantic Coast Fish Stew

Makes 6 servings

4 tablespoons butter
2 tablespoons olive oil
2 medium onions, thinly sliced
3 stalks celery, sliced
2 carrots, sliced
2 cloves garlic, minced
2 cups clam juice
1 can (16 ounces) tomatoes with juice, chopped
2 bay leaves
½ teaspoon salt
½ teaspoon pepper
1½ pounds haddock, hake, scrod or cod, cut into 1½-inch pieces
½ pound scallops
1 pound mussels, debearded
Crusty garlic bread

Heat butter and oil in a stockpot; sauté vegetables and garlic over medium heat, stirring occasionally, until vegetables are tender. Stir in juice, tomatoes and seasonings. Cover and simmer for 4 to 5 minutes. Add haddock; cover with water and simmer for 10 minutes or until fish is cooked. Add scallops and mussels and continue cooking, uncovered, until done, about 6 to 10 minutes. Discard any unopened mussels. Serve in a deep bowl with crusty garlic bread.

Bouillabaisse

Makes 6 to 8 servings

4 tablespoons olive oil
2 onions, thinly sliced
2 leeks, sliced
3 cloves garlic, minced
1 can (28 ounces) tomatoes with liquid, chopped
1 pound haddock, cut into pieces
1 pound red snapper, flounder or monkfish, cut into pieces
1 can (7½ ounces) minced clams with juice
2 cups clam juice
1 pound medium shrimp, shelled and deveined
2 bay leaves
¼ teaspoon thyme
¼ teaspoon fennel seed
¼ teaspoon saffron
Dry white wine
1 pound mussels, debearded
2 tablespoons minced parsley
French bread, sliced
Rouille (see page 63)

Heat olive oil in a stockpot; sauté onions, leeks and garlic until tender. Stir in tomatoes, fish, clams with juice, shrimp, and seasonings. Add wine to cover, if necessary. Simmer, partially covered, stirring occasionally, for 15 minutes. Add remaining ingredients except bread and Rouille. Cover and simmer 10 minutes or until mussels are cooked. Remove and discard bay leaves and any unopened mussels. Serve in deep bowls with French bread and Rouille.

Chicken Marengo

Makes 5 to 6 servings

2 tablespoons butter
2 tablespoons olive oil
1 3½ to 4-pound chicken, cut into
   8 pieces
   Salt, pepper and garlic powder
   to taste
1 large onion, sliced
1 can (16 ounces) tomatoes with
   juice, chopped
½ cup chicken stock
¼ cup dry red wine
¼ teaspoon thyme
1 pound mushrooms, sliced
1 cup stuffed green olives
   Buttered noodles

Heat butter and olive oil in a large heavy skillet. Sprinkle chicken with salt, pepper and garlic powder; add to skillet, skin-side-down, and brown. Turn chicken and add onion; cook until chicken is tender and browned. Stir in remaining ingredients; cover and simmer 45 minutes. Add additional stock, if necessary. Arrange hot buttered noodles on a serving platter; top with chicken, vegetables and sauce. Serve hot.

Couscous

Makes 8 servings

½ cup butter
2 3½-pound chickens, cut into
   serving pieces
3 tablespoons olive oil
2 onions, sliced
2 cloves garlic, minced
3 large ripe tomatoes, peeled and
   sliced
1 can (15½ ounces) chick peas,
   drained
3 carrots, sliced
½ head medium cabbage, cut into
   wedges
1 turnip, sliced
½ teaspoon paprika
½ teaspoon salt
½ teaspoon cinnamon
½ teaspoon ginger
½ teaspoon saffron
½ teaspoon pepper
½ teaspoon cumin
½ cup dark raisins
   Chicken stock
1 pound instant *or* regular
   couscous, cooked

Melt butter in a stockpot or "couscoussier." Brown chicken; remove and reserve. Add oil to drippings and sauté onions and garlic until tender. Mix in remaining vegetables, seasonings and raisins. Add stock to cover vegetables. Return chicken to pot. Simmer, partially covered, 45 minutes or until chicken and vegetables are cooked. Mound couscous in center of large platter. Arrange chicken and vegetables around the couscous. Serve hot.

Brunswick Stew

Makes 6 servings

4 tablespoons bacon drippings
2 large onions, thinly sliced
3½ pounds chicken, cut into serving
    pieces
¼ teaspoon salt
¼ teaspoon pepper
¼ teaspoon garlic powder
4 tomatoes, peeled and chopped
¼ cup dry sherry
1 teaspoon Worcestershire sauce
2 packages (10 ounces each)
    frozen lima beans, thawed
1 package (10 ounces) frozen
    okra, thawed
1 package (10 ounces) frozen
    corn, thawed
3 tablespoons butter
½ cup seasoned dry bread crumbs

Heat bacon drippings in Dutch oven over medium heat. Sauté onions, stirring occasionally, until tender. Brown chicken and add seasonings. Add 2 cups boiling water, tomatoes, sherry and Worcestershire sauce. Simmer, partially covered, for 30 minutes. Add remaining ingredients except butter and crumbs. Simmer, stirring occasionally, for 45 minutes or until tender. Stir butter into stew. Stir in bread crumbs and simmer 20 minutes. Serve in deep bowls.

Veal Stew

Makes 8 servings

1½ pounds veal shoulder, cut into
    1-inch pieces
1½ pounds veal breast, cut into
    1½-inch pieces
4 tablespoons butter
1 quart veal stock
2 large onions, minced
2 carrots, sliced
4 stalks celery, diced
1 clove garlic, minced
¼ teaspoon cloves
    Salt and pepper to taste
½ cup dry white wine
2 cups whole mushrooms
¼ cup butter
¼ cup flour
3 egg yolks, beaten
½ cup heavy cream
2 tablespoons freshly squeezed
    lemon juice
    Buttered noodles

Blanch veal shoulder and breast in salted water; drain and rinse under cold water. Melt butter in a large heavy saucepan; add stock, onions, carrots, celery, seasonings and wine. Simmer, uncovered, 1¼ to 1½ hours or until veal is tender. Add mushrooms during last 10 minutes of cooking. Remove vegetables from stock with a slotted spoon. In a small saucepan, melt butter; whisk in flour until absorbed. Whisk mixture into veal and simmer, stirring often, for 10 minutes. Remove from heat; return vegetables. Combine egg yolks and cream; stir in 2 tablespoons of veal stock and return to stew. Stir in lemon juice. Adjust seasonings. Serve over buttered noodles.

Osso Buco (Stewed Veal Shanks)

Makes 6 servings

½ cup flour
½ teaspoon salt
¼ teaspoon freshly ground black
    pepper
6 veal shanks, chopped in pieces
¼ cup olive oil
2 large onions, sliced
3 stalks celery, sliced
4 carrots, sliced
2 cloves garlic, minced
½ teaspoon tarragon
½ teaspoon thyme
3 bay leaves
¼ cup chopped parsley
1½ cups veal stock
6 ripe tomatoes, peeled and
    chopped or 2 cans (16 ounces
    each) tomatoes with juice
    Cooked rice or noodles

Combine flour, salt and pepper. Coat veal lightly with flour. Heat oil in a large heavy skillet; brown veal and transfer to a plate. Reheat oil and sauté vegetables until tender. Stir in seasonings and return veal. Add stock and cook over medium heat for 10 minutes. Add tomatoes and simmer, partially covered, stirring occasionally, for 2 hours. Add additional veal stock, if necessary. Serve over rice.

Stew in a Pumpkin

Makes 6 to 8 servings

3 tablespoons butter
2 pounds rump roast, cut into
    1-inch pieces
3 tablespoons cornstarch
2 large onions, minced
3 tomatoes, chopped
2 tablespoons butter
¼ teaspoon salt
¼ teaspoon pepper
3 cups beef stock
½ pound prunes
½ pound dried apricots
3 sweet potatoes, sliced
2 packages (10 ounces each)
    frozen corn, thawed and drained
1 pumpkin, cut top off and reserve,
    discard seeds and membrane

Melt butter in a Dutch oven. Roll meat in cornstarch. Sauté meat until brown; set aside. In a separate skillet, sauté vegetables in butter until tender; add to meat. Sprinkle with salt and pepper. Stir in remaining ingredients except pumpkin. Cover and simmer for 1 hour. Preheat oven to 325°. Ladle stew into prepared pumpkin. Carefully place pumpkin in a roasting pan and bake 1 hour. Using pot holders, carefully transfer pumpkin to serving platter. Serve stew from pumpkin with ladle.

Beef Goulash

Makes 6 to 8 servings

3½ pounds chuck steak, cut into
    1-inch pieces
½ cup flour
4 tablespoons vegetable oil
3 onions, chopped
2 green bell peppers, sliced
3 cloves garlic, minced
1 can (16 ounces) tomatoes with
    juice, chopped
1 can (6 ounces) tomato paste
2 large tomatoes, peeled and
    cubed
¾ cup beef stock
1 teaspoon paprika
½ teaspoon salt
½ teaspoon thyme
½ teaspoon caraway seeds
¼ teaspoon pepper
1½ cups sour cream
    Hot buttered noodles

Dust meat with flour. Heat oil in Dutch oven; brown meat until flour is absorbed. Add vegetables, stock and spices. Cover and simmer, stirring occasionally, for 1½ hours. Uncover and cook, stirring often, for 30 minutes or until meat is tender. Blend in sour cream and warm, but *do not boil.* Serve over hot buttered noodles.

Oxtail Stew

Makes 6 servings

5 pounds oxtails, disjointed
1 cup flour
½ teaspoon salt
¼ teaspoon freshly ground pepper
4 strips bacon, cut into 1-inch
    pieces
1 large onion, sliced
2 carrots, sliced
2 leeks, sliced
3 turnips, quartered
2 bay leaves
½ teaspoon thyme
½ teaspoon cloves
1 can (16 ounces) tomatoes with
    juice
2 cups beef bouillon
2 cups dry red wine

Wash oxtails and pat dry. Combine flour, salt and pepper on a sheet of waxed paper. Coat oxtails with flour mixture. Fry bacon in a stockpot; remove all but 4 tablespoons of the drippings. Add oxtails and brown on all sides over medium-high heat. Add onion, carrots, leeks and turnips; mix well. Add remaining ingredients; bring to a boil. Reduce heat and simmer, partially covered, stirring occasionally, for 2 hours. Remove and discard bay leaves. Serve in deep bowls.

CHILLED SOUPS

No-Cook Tomato Soup

Makes 6 servings

4½ cups tomato juice
3 green onions, minced
2 cups heavy cream *or* half-and-half, stiffly beaten
¼ teaspoon garlic powder
2 bay leaves
Chopped basil, optional

Combine all ingredients except basil in a deep bowl. Cover and chill for 1 hour. Discard bay leaves. Ladle soup into bowls and garnish with chopped basil, if desired.

Gazpacho Andaluz

Makes 5 to 6 servings

3 large ripe tomatoes, peeled and chopped
1 green bell pepper, diced
1 cucumber, peeled and sliced
1 tablespoon catsup
4 green onions, chopped
1 clove garlic, minced
¼ teaspoon cumin
2 tablespoons red wine vinegar
2 tablespoons mayonnaise
3 cups chicken stock
1 cup bread crumbs
¼ teaspoon salt
¼ teaspoon pepper
Chopped tomato
Chopped green pepper
Chopped cucumber

Combine all ingredients in a blender or food processor except the chopped tomato, pepper and cucumber; process until smooth. Cover and chill for 1 hour. To serve, stir soup and top individual servings with chopped vegetables.

Melon Soup

Makes 6 servings

3 small melons, remove pulp and freeze shells
½ cup dry white wine
½ cup freshly squeezed orange juice
1 cup heavy cream, whipped
¼ cup sugar
1 orange, thinly sliced
Nutmeg *or* cinnamon

Purée melon pulp; blend in remaining ingredients except orange and nutmeg. Cover and chill until ready to serve. Serve soup in frozen melon shells; garnish with orange slices and a dash of nutmeg.

Fruit Soup

Makes 6 servings

3 cups freshly squeezed orange
   juice
2 plums, coarsely chopped
4 peaches, coarsely chopped
2 tablespoons freshly squeezed
   lemon juice
2 large bananas, sliced
3 apples, chopped
2 tablespoons grated orange rind
   Yogurt

Lightly process all ingredients, except yogurt, in a blender or food processor. Cover and chill. Serve in chilled glasses and garnish with yogurt.

Pea Soup

Makes 6 servings

3 tablespoons butter
2 onions, minced
3 potatoes, diced
2 pounds fresh green peas *or*
   3 packages (10 ounces each)
   frozen peas, thawed
1 tablespoon salt
2 tablespoons butter
   Salt and white pepper to taste
1 teaspoon chopped mint leaves
2 cups milk
1 cup heavy cream
   Mint leaves

Melt butter in a saucepan; sauté onions until tender. Stir in potatoes and 1 cup boiling water; cover and cook until potatoes are tender, about 15 minutes. Cook peas until tender with salt and 1 cup boiling water; drain. Purée vegetables and transfer to a saucepan with butter and seasonings. Blend in milk over low heat, adding more milk, if necessary, until soup is of desired consistency. Cover and refrigerate until ready to serve. Just before serving, stir in cream and garnish with mint leaves.

Blueberry-Yogurt Soup

Makes 6 servings

1 package (16 ounces) frozen
   blueberries, at room temperature
4 cups blueberry yogurt
¼ cup sugar
¼ teaspoon cinnamon
   Dash ginger
   Flaked coconut
   Mint sprigs, optional

In a deep mixing bowl, blend all ingredients except coconut and mint until smooth. Cover and refrigerate until ready to serve. Garnish with flaked coconut and sprigs of mint, if desired.

No-Cook Peach Soup

Makes 4 servings

3 cups freshly peeled and chopped peaches with juice
2 cups peach juice
1 cup sour cream
½ teaspoon cinnamon
¼ cup sliced toasted almonds

Purée peaches and place in a deep bowl. Stir in remaining ingredients except toasted almonds. Cover and chill for 1 hour. Serve with additional sour cream and sprinkle with almonds.

Coconut-Curry Soup

Makes 6 servings

3 tablespoons butter
2 large onions, thinly sliced
1 clove garlic, minced
1 tablespoon flour
½ teaspoon curry powder
5 cups chicken stock
2 large tomatoes, peeled and chopped
2 apples, chopped
2 tablespoons freshly grated coconut
1 lime, thinly sliced
2 cups half-and-half
Grated coconut

Melt butter in a large saucepan. Sauté onions and garlic until tender. Whisk in flour and curry powder until absorbed. Stir in remaining ingredients except half-and-half and coconut. Cover and simmer for ½ hour. Strain soup into a large bowl; cool. Add half-and-half; mix well. Cover and chill until ready to serve. Sprinkle with coconut.

Yogurt-Grape Soup

Makes 6 servings

1 cup chopped seedless red grapes
1 cup chopped seedless green grapes
½ cup chopped walnuts
½ cup chopped celery
3 cups lemon yogurt
Sunflower seeds

Combine all ingredients except yogurt and sunflower seeds in a mixing bowl. Cover and chill for 20 minutes. In a bowl, stir yogurt until smooth; blend in grape mixture. Pour soup into shallow serving bowls and serve immediately. Garnish with sunflower seeds.

It's the Berries

Makes 6 servings

1 quart strawberries, hulled
2 cups raspberries
½ teaspoon cinnamon
¼ teaspoon nutmeg
1 cup sugar
2 cups water *or* berry juice
½ cup sweet red wine
1 cup strawberry soda
Sweetened whipped cream
1 cup sliced strawberries
Fresh mint leaves

Blend together strawberries, raspberries, cinnamon, nutmeg, sugar and water in a saucepan; bring to a boil. Reduce heat and simmer, stirring often, until sugar is dissolved, about 3 to 4 minutes. Cool soup, purée and place in a deep bowl. Stir in wine and soda. Cover and refrigerate soup until ready to serve. Garnish with whipped cream, sliced strawberries and mint leaves.

Beet Soup

Makes 6 servings

2 cans (16 ounces each) diced beets with juice
1 tablespoon honey
3 tablespoons freshly squeezed lemon juice
Salt to taste
3 to 4 eggs, beaten
6 medium potatoes, boiled
½ cup chopped green onions
2 cups sour cream *or* yogurt

Combine beets and honey in a medium saucepan; bring to a boil over high heat. Stir in lemon juice. Reduce heat and simmer for 10 minutes or until tender. Cool soup to room temperature; purée. Add salt. Add eggs to soup in a slow steady stream. Cover and refrigerate until chilled. To serve, place a hot potato in each bowl. Ladle soup around potato, sprinkle with chopped green onions and pass sour cream at table.

Avocado Soup

Makes 6 servings

6 ripe avocados, mashed
3 cloves garlic, minced
2 tablespoons freshly squeezed lime juice
1½ quarts chicken stock
1 cup sour cream
¼ teaspoon salt
¼ teaspoon white pepper
Toasted slivered almonds

Combine avocados, garlic, lime juice and stock; blend well. Stir in sour cream and season to taste with salt and pepper. Pour into compotes or bowls and sprinkle with almonds.

It's the Berries, this page

Artichoke Soup

Makes 6 servings

2 tablespoons butter
3 stalks celery, chopped
1 can (14 ounces) artichoke
  bottoms, drained
4 cups chicken stock
¼ teaspoon salt
¼ teaspoon white pepper
¼ teaspoon ginger
3 tablespoons dry white wine
1 cup heavy cream
  Chopped walnuts

Melt butter in a medium heavy saucepan. Sauté celery until tender. Add artichoke bottoms and cook, stirring often, for 3 minutes; cool and purée. Return purée to saucepan. Add stock, seasonings and wine. Simmer 10 minutes, uncovered; chill. Whip cream until stiff peaks form; fold into soup. Sprinkle with walnuts and serve.

Iced Cranberry Soup

Makes 6 to 8 servings

1 cup pineapple juice
½ cup sugar
2 cups dry sherry
1 pound cranberries
2 tablespoons butter
1 tablespoon grated orange rind
1 cup heavy cream
2 cups sour cream
  Chopped walnuts

Combine pineapple juice, sugar and sherry in a saucepan; bring to a boil over medium heat. Stir in cranberries and return mixture to a boil. Reduce heat and simmer for 5 minutes. Let berries stand for 10 minutes; stir. Refrigerate until cold. Heat butter in skillet and stir in orange rind; add to cranberries and purée. Blend in cream and 1 cup of the sour cream. Ladle into small bowls; garnish with remaining sour cream and walnuts.

Chilled Sorrel Soup

Makes 8 servings

2 pounds sorrel, stems removed,
  chopped
2 tablespoons freshly squeezed
  lemon juice
3 tablespoons sugar
2 eggs, slightly beaten
1 teaspoon salt
1 cucumber, chopped
1 cup sour cream

Bring 2 quarts water to a boil in a large saucepan over high heat. Add sorrel and boil for 2 minutes. Reduce heat and simmer for 10 minutes. Stir in lemon juice and sugar; cook 2 minutes longer. Remove soup from heat, cool slightly. In a large mixing bowl, combine eggs with salt; stir into soup in a slow steady stream. Cool soup and chill until ready to serve. Serve in shallow bowls with chopped cucumber and sour cream.

Cucumber Soup
Makes 6 servings

3 medium cucumbers, coarsely chopped
1 onion, minced
1 clove garlic, minced
¼ teaspoon white pepper
½ teaspoon salt
¼ teaspoon white pepper
2 cups chicken stock
2 cups plain yogurt
½ cup chopped walnuts
Chopped dill

Combine vegetables, seasonings and stock in a blender; purée. Stir in yogurt. Cover and chill until ready to serve. Serve in coffee mugs, sprinkled with walnuts and dill.

Cherry Soup with Almonds
Makes 6 servings

2 cans (16 ounces each) pitted sweet black cherries with juice
½ cup sugar
1 tablespoon cornstarch mixed with 4 tablespoons of the cherry juice
¼ teaspoon cinnamon
¼ teaspoon nutmeg
½ cup sweet red wine
½ cup ground almonds
¼ cup toasted slivered almonds
Sweetened whipped cream

Chop cherries coarsely. In a medium saucepan, combine cherries with juice, sugar, cornstarch mixture and spices. Simmer, uncovered, stirring often, until soup thickens slightly. Remove soup from heat and stir in wine and almonds. Cover and refrigerate until chilled. Serve sprinkled with slivered almonds and topped with whipped cream.

Apple-Cinnamon Soup
Makes 6 servings

3 tablespoons butter
1 large red onion, minced
4 large firm cooking apples, unpeeled and chopped
1 quart chicken stock
¼ teaspoon salt
¼ teaspoon nutmeg
¼ teaspoon cinnamon
2 cups half-and-half or heavy cream
½ cup chopped hazelnuts or walnuts

Melt butter in a large heavy saucepan. Sauté onion and apples over medium-high heat, until tender. Add stock and seasonings; blend. Simmer 10 minutes, partially covered. Fold in half-and-half; warm. Chill until ready to serve. Sprinkle with chopped hazelnuts and serve.

STOCK AND CONSOMMÉ

Veal Stock

Makes 3 to 4 cups

4 pounds veal bones
1 onion, chopped
1 clove garlic, crushed
1 carrot, sliced
1 stalk celery, sliced
½ teaspoon salt
½ teaspoon freshly ground pepper

Roast bones in 325° oven for 45 minutes. Combine bones and remaining ingredients in a stockpot; add 1 gallon of water. Bring stock to a boil; reduce heat and simmer for 1½ to 2 hours. Strain stock and skim. Return stock to pot and simmer for 1 hour or until stock is reduced to 3 or 4 cups. Cover and refrigerate until needed.

Consommé

Makes 3 cups

1 quart chicken stock
2 teaspoons tomato paste
¼ cup dry sherry
2 egg whites, stiffly beaten
2 eggshells, crushed

Arrange all ingredients except egg whites and shells in a large heavy saucepan. Heat to simmer. Add egg whites and shells; bring soup to a rolling boil. Remove soup from heat and cool for 15 minutes. Line a colander with a double layer of cheesecloth and place over a deep bowl; strain soup.

Jellied Consommé

Makes 6 servings

1 envelope unflavored gelatin
2 cans (10½ ounces each) consommé
Dash Tabasco sauce
1 cup sour cream
Chopped chives

Stir gelatin into ¼-cup cold water. Combine consommé and Tabasco in a medium saucepan. Warm over medium heat. Stir in gelatin mixture until gelatin completely dissolves. Pour consommé into a shallow dish and refrigerate until set. Cut into small cubes or spoon into bowls; top with sour cream and chopped chives.

54

Beef Stock

Makes 3 to 4 cups

4½ pounds beef soup bones, cracked
2 carrots, sliced
2 stalks celery, sliced
3 onions, cut in half, skin left on
1½ pounds chuck steak, cut into pieces
½ teaspoon crushed thyme
2 bay leaves
5 sprigs parsley
5 peppercorns, crushed

Preheat oven to 350°. Arrange soup bones in a shallow pan and roast, turning occasionally, for 45 minutes, or until browned. Combine soup bones, vegetables and meat in a stockpot. Tie seasonings in a piece of cheesecloth and add to stockpot; cover with water. Bring stock to a boil over medium heat. Reduce heat and simmer, uncovered, skimming and adding water as necessary, for 4½ hours. Cool stock and strain through a cheesecloth. Return stock to pan and simmer, uncovered, until reduced by one-third. Cover and store in refrigerator or freezer.

Fish Stock I

Makes 4 to 5 cups

3 tablespoons butter
2 pounds fish bones and head
2 onions, cut in quarters, skin left on
4 stalks celery, sliced
6 sprigs parsley
½ teaspoon whole peppercorns
2 bay leaves

Melt butter in a stockpot; sauté fish bones and head. Add remaining ingredients and cover with water. Bring mixture to a boil over high heat. Reduce heat and simmer, partially covered, for 3½ hours. Skim stock as necessary; cool and strain through a double layer of cheesecloth. Transfer to a covered container and store in refrigerator or freezer.

Fish Stock II

Makes 2 cups

1 medium onion, chopped
2 stalks celery, sliced
1 cup dry white wine
1 pound white-fleshed fish bones
4 black peppercorns
1 bay leaf
3 sprigs parsley

Combine all ingredients in a stockpot. Add water to cover. Simmer, partially covered, over medium heat, for 45 minutes. Skim stock and strain through double layer of cheesecloth. Transfer to a covered container and refrigerate until ready to use.

Mushroom Consommé

Makes 6 servings

1 pound mushrooms, chopped
3 stalks celery, sliced
1 quart chicken stock
2 egg whites, lightly beaten
2 eggshells, crushed
4 tablespoons sherry
¼ teaspoon salt
¼ teaspoon pepper
  Unsweetened whipped cream *or* chopped mushrooms

Combine mushrooms, celery and stock in a heavy saucepan. Simmer, partially covered, for 40 minutes. Strain vegetables through a double layer of cheesecloth over a vegetable strainer. Return liquid to saucepan; add egg whites and shells. Bring soup to a boil and cook for 2 minutes. Strain soup again. Return soup to saucepan and reheat; stir in sherry. Season consommé with salt and pepper and serve garnished with whipped cream or chopped mushrooms.

Chicken Stock I

Makes 3 quarts

1 3½-pound chicken, quartered
2 slices fresh ginger
2 carrots, sliced
2 onions, skin left on
4 stalks celery, tops left on
2 teaspoons salt
½ teaspoon white pepper

Combine all ingredients in a stockpot. Cover with water and bring to a boil. Reduce heat and simmer, covered, for 2 hours. Cool, strain and adjust seasoning. (Reserve chicken for use in salads.) Skim stock and strain. If using for soup, remove and slice vegetables thinly or purée and return to stockpot; reheat and serve with noodles or rice.

Chicken Stock II

Makes 1 quart

4 pounds chicken wings and backs
2 whole onions, skin left on
8 cloves
3 carrots, sliced
1 bunch celery leaves
1 teaspoon tarragon
3 stalks celery, sliced
½ teaspoon crushed peppercorns
3 sprigs parsley
3 sprigs dill

Place chicken in a stockpot and cover with water; bring to a boil over medium heat and skim. Stud onion with cloves and add to stockpot with remaining ingredients. Simmer, partially covered, for 3 hours. Cool and strain stock through cheesecloth.

SOUP ACCOMPANIMENTS

Toasted Croutons

Makes 2 cups

8 slices day-old French bread *or* other white bread
3 tablespoons olive oil

Trim crust from bread; cut into ¼-inch cubes. Heat oil in skillet over medium heat. Add bread cubes and stir constantly until crisp and golden. Drain croutons on a sheet of paper toweling. Use for garnishing soups.

Onion Rings

Makes 6 servings

3 cups flour
3 cups light beer
1 egg
¼ teaspoon garlic powder
Peanut oil for deep-frying
8 medium onions, cut into ¼-inch rings
Salt

In a deep mixing bowl, whisk together flour, beer, egg and garlic powder. Let batter stand at room temperature for 30 minutes; stir. Heat 1 inch of oil to 375° in a large heavy skillet. Dip onion rings into batter and carefully slide into oil; fry until golden, turning once. Drain on paper toweling. Onion rings can be warmed in a 400° oven for 3 to 4 minutes. Sprinkle with salt. Serve warm with soup.

Cheese Straws

Makes 2 dozen

¾ cup flour
¼ teaspoon salt
¼ cup grated sharp Cheddar cheese
¼ cup butter, at room temperature
1 egg yolk, beaten
2 tablespoons ice water

In a deep bowl, combine flour and salt; add cheese and mix. Cut in butter with pastry knife. Blend together egg yolk and water; stir into flour mixture. Gather dough and cover with plastic wrap. Chill for 30 minutes. On a lightly floured surface or pastry cloth, roll dough to a 12 x 4-inch rectangle. Cut crosswise into ½-inch strips. Twist strips and arrange on an ungreased cookie sheet. Bake at 400° for 10 minutes, until cooked. Cool on rack. Store in covered container. Serve in soup.

Tortellini Noodle Dough

Makes 6 servings

2 cups unbleached flour
½ cup instant flour
½ teaspoon salt
3 eggs
2 tablespoons olive oil
1 cup ricotta cheese
¾ cup freshly grated Parmesan cheese
4 tablespoons minced parsley
1 egg yolk
¼ teaspoon salt
¼ teaspoon grated nutmeg
Chicken *or* **beef stock**

Combine flours in a large bowl, making a well in the center. Add salt, eggs and oil; blend and gather into a ball. Knead dough on a lightly floured board until smooth and elastic, about 8 minutes; add flour if necessary. Form dough into a ball and cover with plastic wrap; allow dough to rest for 1 hour.

To make filling, combine remaining ingredients, except stock; set aside. Divide dough into 2 even pieces. Cover ½ of the dough; roll remaining dough on lightly floured surface until paper-thin. Cut dough into 2-inch circles. Spoon ½ teaspoon of filling onto each circle; wet edges with water or beaten egg. Fold in half and pinch edges to seal. Bring stock to a full boil and add tortellini. Reduce heat and continue cooking 15 minutes or until noodles are tender.

Egg Noodles

Makes 6 servings

3 cups flour
½ teaspoon salt
4 eggs
2 tablespoons olive oil
3 tablespoons warm water

Combine flour and salt in a deep mixing bowl; make a well in the center. Mix in remaining ingredients; gather dough into a ball. Knead dough on a lightly floured board, adding flour as necessary, until smooth and elastic, about 6 to 8 minutes. Form dough into a ball and cover with plastic wrap; allow to rest for 1 hour. Divide dough into 4 pieces. Using one piece of dough at a time, roll on a lightly floured board until 1½ inches in thickness. Quickly roll dough up in jelly roll fashion; cut crosswise into ¼-inch slices. Unroll noodles, cook immediately in salted boiling water for 3 minutes; drain. Serve in soup.

Note: Noodles can be frozen in plastic bags.

Meat Turnovers

Makes 3 dozen

2 cups flour
½ teaspoon salt
½ teaspoon baking powder
¼ cup butter, cut in pieces
1 egg, slightly beaten
½ cup sour cream
1 egg yolk
1 tablespoon water
2 tablespoons butter
1 pound ground meat
3 green onions, minced
¼ teaspoon salt
¼ teaspoon pepper
2 teaspoons flour
1 cup sour cream
   Fresh dill sprigs

Combine flour, salt, baking powder and butter in a large bowl of electric mixer; process until mixture resembles rough corn meal. Blend in egg and sour cream. Gather dough together, wrap in plastic wrap and chill for 1 hour.

Beat together egg yolk and water; set aside. To make filling, heat butter in heavy skillet; add ground meat, onions, salt and pepper. Sauté until meat loses its color, stirring occasionally. Stir in flour until absorbed; cool and set aside. Roll out chilled dough on lightly floured cloth until ¼-inch thick; cut into 3-inch circles. Spoon 1 teaspoon of filling onto each circle; fold in half and pinch edges to seal. Glaze with egg yolk mixture. Place turnovers on greased and floured cookie sheet. Bake in preheated 375° oven for 30 minutes. Garnish turnovers with sour cream and fresh dill sprigs. Serve hot with soup.

Chicken Quenelles

Makes 2 dozen

1 1-pound chicken breast, skinned, boned and cubed
½ teaspoon salt
½ teaspoon freshly ground pepper
¼ teaspoon nutmeg
1 tablespoon minced parsley
2 egg whites, lightly beaten
2 cups heavy cream
1 tablespoon butter
   Salted hot water

Purée chicken and seasonings in a food processor fitted with a steel blade or in a grinder with a fine blade. Transfer to a mixing bowl. Beat in egg whites. Add cream by tablespoons until the mixture holds its shape. Butter a large heavy skillet. Dip 2 tablespoons into hot water. Shape mixture into egg-shaped dumplings with the hot tablespoons. Slide quenelles into the buttered skillet; do not crowd pan. Add salted hot water until quenelles float. Bring water to a simmer and continue cooking until quenelles are firm, about 6 to 8 minutes. Remove with a slotted spoon; serve in soup.

Dumplings
Makes 6 to 8 servings

1 egg, slightly beaten
¾ cup flour
  Salt and white pepper to taste

Combine dumpling ingredients in a bowl. Bring 1 quart water to a boil in a saucepan. Drop teaspoonfuls of dough into the water. Reduce heat to simmer and continue cooking for 3 minutes or until cooked. Strain dumplings and add to soup.

Rouille
Makes 1 cup

4 cloves garlic, crushed
1 cup fresh bread crumbs
¾ cup sliced roasted red bell pepper
2 teaspoons tomato paste
¼ teaspoon cayenne
¼ teaspoon paprika
¼ cup olive oil

Using a blender or food processor fitted with a steel blade, purée all ingredients except olive oil. With machine running, pour olive oil through the feed tube in a slow steady stream until blended. Cover and refrigerate. Use for seasoning soups.

Spaetzle
Makes 4 to 6 servings

1 cup flour
1 egg
½ teaspoon salt
½ cup milk

Combine flour, egg and salt together in a mixing bowl. Add milk in a slow steady stream, stirring until batter is smooth and thin. Let batter stand for 10 minutes; stir. Bring a large pot of salted water to a rolling boil over medium-high heat. Press teaspoonfuls of batter through the holes of a coarse colander into the boiling water. Boil rapidly for 8 minutes, until cooked. Drain, rinse and serve in hot soup.

Index